FREEDOM IN
PIANO TECHNIQUE

FREEDOM IN PIANO TECHNIQUE

by

JOAN LAST

HAMMOND TEXTBOOKS

Printed in the EU

Order No. HAM020
ISBN 1-84609-504-2

FOREWORD

Anyone who is bold enough to write about piano technique must be prepared for criticism and disagreement. There is more than one recognized school of technique, and a pianist may achieve speed or tonal beauty by means that seem foreign to an equally gifted colleague. Let me say, then, that I am offering *one* simple and straightforward way of gaining ease and enjoyment in piano playing.

The great 'technical thinker' Tobias Matthay was looked upon by some as a revolutionary, as are all forward-thinking people. Today the core of his principles lives on, and his deeply perceptive analysis of the movements of arms, hands, and fingers has contributed in no small way to the astonishing facility of today's younger pianists. Of course it needs more than technique to gain a place at the top, but technique is at least a means of conveying musical insight to the public.

In my childhood the number of 'names' in the solo performing world was less overwhelming than today. The great 'giants of the keyboard' travelled the world in a leisurely way, often accompanied by their own concert grand pianos. They could survive for a season on a limited repertoire repeated at each country visited. Today's successful pianists need almost superhuman speed of learning and the ability to retain and perform at short notice innumerable concertos and recital programmes. They need, too, supreme dedication and a strong physique if they are to survive the stresses imposed by continuous jet travel from one part of the world to another.

Matthay, with his deeply questing and perceptive mind, wrote in great detail. He propounded facts as would a surgeon whose students need to have a complete knowledge of the anatomy of the body in order to pass a stiff examination. Compared with him I humbly offer simple First Aid, hoping to help even the near beginner to play, before too long, with a measure of freedom and enjoyment. However, what I have to say is not concerned only with the early stages of piano playing. I hope to involve and interest progressing pianists, teachers, and students who are working for a Teacher's Piano Diploma. Many candidates for these examinations worry about the questions on technique and may give answers that are somewhat hazy or confused. To them I offer something simple, basic, and very much to the point. A special summing up of their needs appears at the end of the book.

For my purpose a long book is not needed and I hope its very brevity will encourage my readers. If I were asked to sum up in one word the purpose behind my thinking I would say 'freedom'. This replaces the more elusive 'relaxation' used by Matthay, to which I refer later.

Matthay himself found nothing unusual in his ideas. To him they were a natural process which led to complete freedom. His reaction to those who wanted his advice can be illustrated in the following anecdote. One day a lady applied for a consultation lesson, explaining that she had not come to play to him but to ask him about his method. 'Method,' replied Matthay, 'I haven't got one.' Slightly taken aback, the lady persevered. 'Well, do you think you could show me the system by which you teach technique?' 'Madam,' replied Matthay, 'I don't teach a method or a system, I teach *common sense.*'

In a more modest way my aim is to do just that.

J.L.

CONTENTS

Dedicated to Alison Baker after seven years of shared experience in piano playing. My thanks are due to her for posing for the photographs and to Joanna Lynn for Plate 15.

1. UNDERSTANDING THE INSTRUMENT

The pianist needs a basic knowledge of the workings of his instrument if he is to appreciate what sort of skill and sensitivity it will demand from his arms, hands, and fingers. Piano tone is produced in a way totally unlike that of its predecessor, the harpsichord, neither does its action bear any resemblance to that of the organ.

The harpsichord has a set of horizontal strings which are plucked, whereas those of the piano are struck. The harpsichordist is unable to alter tonal amount or quality by finger skill: this is accomplished by changing from one manual (keyboard) to another, or by pedals which cause different sets of strings to come into action.

The organ, the largest and most complex of the keyboard instruments, can sound an almost overwhelming permutation of notes through as many as four or even five manuals plus a pedal keyboard. Tonal quality and quantity are determined by a complicated set of stops and swells. Thus, the organist relies on mechanical means to serve his purpose *tonally*, no effect beyond 'legato' or 'detached' articulation being got through the fingers. One cannot speak of an organist as having a 'lovely touch'.

The piano is therefore the most intimate of these keyboard instruments, able to reflect musical character through the sensitive skill and control of the *fingers*. This is what technique is all about. I sincerely hope that a future generation will not add sets of gadgets or gimmicks to produce sounds as from an organ or harpsichord. Some such efforts have been made, but luckily with no lasting impact!

What then does the pianist need to know about his instrument?

I propose to give only the simplest description of the basic mechanism. Further information can be gained from books specializing in the subject.

As the shape of a grand piano immediately suggests, its frame is harp-like in construction so that the strings may be graded in size, the long thick strings belonging to the lower notes and the short thin strings to the higher. On an upright piano the 'harp' is of course perpendicular. In both, the strings are stretched over a soundboard, which acts as a resonator. To ensure balance between higher and lower notes we find only one string for each note of the lowest octave, two strings for a little more than the second octave, and, from then on, three strings for each note. During the 19th century 'overstringing' was introduced and is now normal. By this method one longer group of strings is made to cross another, more or less diagonally, so that the required length of string can be fitted into a reasonably sized instrument.

Now we come to the key. It leads to a felt-covered 'hammer'. When we strike the key it acts as the lower end of a see-saw, causing the hammer to fly up and strike the strings. (In an upright piano the hammer flies forward.) Immediately it has touched the strings it falls back a little way, leaving them free to vibrate. When the key is completely released the hammer drops back to its original position in line with the other hammers.

Equally important are the dampers – a row of felts which rest on the strings when the piano is not in action. Looking inside the instrument we see that they are longer and thicker for the bass notes and shorter and thinner in the treble. This is in accordance with the vibrational speed of each note. Being short and thin, the very highest strings require no dampers at all, for the sound stops almost as the key is lifted. When a key is struck, the damper connected with that particular key moves away, allowing the strings to vibrate. At the moment the key is released the damper falls back into place. The sustaining pedal (or damper pedal) is directly connected with damper action and, with all pianists except beginners, plays a vital part in interpretation. This is the right-hand pedal. It must on no account be called the 'loud pedal': in fact it can serve to 'cloud' or beautify the very softest passages. When depressed it causes *all the dampers* to release their hold on the strings, causing resonance throughout the range of the instrument. Even the higher strings, which have no dampers, can be set into resonance by 'sympathetic vibration'. Needless to say skill is needed in the use of such an influential part of the mechanism. It has been called the 'soul' of the piano, its first function being to join sounds that cannot be reached with the fingers, but even more, to add richness and beauty to the tone. There are many subtle ways in which the sustaining pedal can be directed. Chapter 14 deals with this in detail.

Beyond these permanently active mechanisms there is the soft pedal – the left-hand one. This, when depressed, causes the keys and action of the grand piano to move to the right. By this means the hammers strike two instead of three strings (the strings being part of the fixed frame) and make contact with a less worn part of the felt. On most upright pianos the use of the soft pedal brings the hammers closer to the strings so that they strike them with less speed.

Finally there is the middle pedal found on concert grands. Its purpose is to sustain a lower note or chord which is to be held as a continuous bass whilst the upper voices have changing harmonies. For successful action this pedal has to be depressed *just after* the required low chord is struck. It can be very effective indeed, but since few pianists have access to it for practising, it is not widely used.

Here, then, we have at our fingertips an instrument of incredible complexity, the result of centuries of research, expertise, and skill. It is for the pianist to make the most of its great potential and, assuming our instrument is in reasonable condition, to coax from it all the beauty of which it is capable.

2. FREEDOM

Having said in my foreword that the main idea behind my technical thinking is 'freedom', I now seek to expand this further. Freedom, in everyday life, is something for which everyone hopes. We speak of freedom from worry or ill-health or any other unpleasant state. When we speak of freedom of speech and action, we imply a lack of restraint. Freedom in piano technique is, similarly, lack of physical restraint. It is basic to much that Matthay wrote, and for it he used the word 'relaxation'.

The stress of everyday living causes people to read books or attend classes on 'how to relax'. One well-known process is to lie down and, concentrating on every part of the body from toes to head, first tense and then relax that part. Relaxation in piano playing can hardly be as complete as that – even though Diploma candidates have on occasions been known to tell astonished examiners that pianists should relax *everything*! Were we to do that we would remain prone on the ground! But let us assume we have exerted the muscles that enable us to get up and sit in front of the piano. What next? Our first action is to raise the hands by exerting the *shoulder muscles*. The shoulder always supports the arm and should never be relaxed. (Neither should it be hunched up into stiffness, sometimes caused by anxiety.)

A rather pedantic, but completely accurate, sentence has been used to describe the relative condition of hands and arms: 'The arm should be self-supporting, equally balanced between shoulder and finger-tip.' In spite of its rather self-conscious wording it does imply in a very direct way

1 *Balanced sitting position*

that the two constantly exerted parts are the shoulder and the finger-tip, or pad. This pad should never lose its 'objective feel' for the keys, and in the end becomes the most sensitive part of tone production at all levels.

Between the shoulders and fingers the muscles in the arms and hands must respond to quick brain directions, according to the technical requirements of the music. These responses eventually become spontaneous, but such a desirable state takes years of practice.

Each movable lever in the body has two sets of muscles, one pulling in one direction and the other in opposition. If you raise the whole arm so that the hand is held at shoulder level and maintain the position for a few seconds, the arm is held up by the activity of the upward shoulder muscles and the passivity of the 'down' muscles. Let the 'up' muscles relax and the arm will start to fall downward. Were the same muscles quickly to reassert themselves the arm would be arrested on the way down. The answer, then, to 'What do we relax?' is 'any muscles not needed for the job of the moment'.

From the time we get up in the morning (assuming all our working parts are in order) the brain transmits a series of messages to the active muscles required to wash, brush our hair, put on our clothes, or even cook the breakfast! These movements do not need to be thought out, being directed by 'muscular memory'. But when an unaccustomed activity, such as playing the piano, is first introduced the brain has to give instructions to fingers and arms. If these are indecisive, opposite sets of muscles may come into conflict. Therefore the pianist needs to acquire a knowledge of the directional movements involved, whatever the technical demands of the music.

The first thing is to adopt a good sitting position and easy hand shape. The height at which we sit may vary, but the most generally accepted and practical is one in which, when the arm is held towards the keyboard, the elbow is in line with the knuckles. The wrist, being flexible, drops very slightly, so that there is slope from it up to the knuckles, from which the fingers work downwards to the keys. Unfortunately many students do not have movable stools and tend to use whatever is available. It would be much better if they took the trouble to alter the height, either by adding hard, firm cushions or (a more drastic measure) by asking the nearest carpenter to saw a little off the legs of chair or stool! The piano stools that one buys are nearly always far too high and excessive height will cause problems with arm flexibility and tone control.

An acceptable hand position is as it falls naturally at one's side, the fingers neither straight nor 'crunched up'. This position can also be formed by sitting with the hands grasping the knees and, retaining that shape, lifting them to the keys.

The worst possible tension is caused by an arched wrist and caved-in knuckles.

Proof of this tension can be got by holding the hand forward, with the wrist arched and held firmly up, whilst the fingers are bent and drawn backwards as far as they can go. Such a position will cause immense problems as more is demanded of the technique. The habit is extremely difficult to break if allowed to continue through several grades. It may be due to an over-insistence on 'round fingers' to the exclusion of all else, probably in the beginning stages. Once a pupil who had already reached Grade 8 came to me in this state. I spent two years trying to eradicate the fault, but it was so ingrained that she was *never* able to play with real facility or produce big tone. Naturally we do not want our beginners to play with flat fingers: the word should be 'curved' rather than 'round', bringing the pad of the finger, rather than the finger nail, into contact with the notes. It must be accepted that, as the stretch is required to extend, the fingers become less curved (see Plates 2–4).

2 *'Easy' hand shape*

3 *The fingers become less curved with a wider span*

Equally important with height is distance from the keyboard. Many pianists sit far too close, impeding free movement over the range of the instrument. A good check is to reach for the highest note with the left hand, followed immediately by the lowest note with the right hand. If these

can be played without leaning backwards or causing dis-
comfort, then the distance is good.

Another point, about which I in my own teaching am
adamant, is that no pianist should sit on 'the whole of the
stool'. There may be some physical reason why no alterna-
tive is possible – the child who cannot reach the floor with

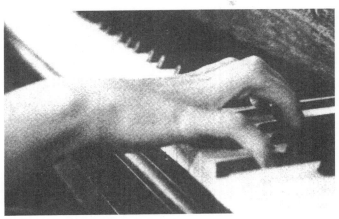

4 *Uneasy and tense hand shape*

his feet is bound to sit fairly and squarely to feel securely
balanced (an ideal is a footstool, but ideals are not always
easy to carry out). The growing child should be encouraged
to reach the floor with his feet as soon as possible by sitting
well forward on the stool. Apart from control of the pedal
when the time comes, he will have greater security in
spanning a wide area of the keyboard. If you doubt this, try
sitting very close to the keyboard firmly on the whole seat
with the feet on the ground. Now stretch out to the right,
grasping the piano frame with the right hand beyond the
top of the highest key, and swing that elbow out in a line
with the hand. From this position, using the palm of the
hand to push off, swing to the left and adopt a similar
position. Continue swinging from side to side and it is likely

you will lose your balance, or at least the anchorage of your feet! So push the stool away, sit on about two-thirds of it and repeat the swinging exercise. You will find that it can now be done with ease. I have introduced this idea to many quite advanced students who have been delighted with the added ease of their new sitting position. Of course, 'sitting away' results in the body leaning *slightly* towards the piano from the base of the spine to the shoulders. This seems to me to be an asset for the body plays a part in controlling the movements of arms and fingers and can hardly do this if it is held erect and rigid (see Plate 1).

Finally let us make sure the legs are neither sprawled at an awkward angle nor crossed. The most natural position is towards the pedals, the right foot a little forward from the left.

There are pianists of distinction whose posture is not exactly as I have described and who yet have marvellous tone production and ease of movement – as I have already said there is more than one school of thought about piano technique. But I do think, in all sincerity, that I am offering one that is practical and helpful.

By now many of my readers will be thinking: 'This is all very well, but what about *finger action*?' Of course it is all-important. But fingers can only function with ease if the supporting mechanism allows them to. I have started from where movement *begins* rather than (as in my own early lessons) where it *ends*. Fifty years ago first lessons were entirely directed at the fingers and I have an indelible memory of Schmitt's many permutations of the five-note compass. Nor were *pieces* allowed to stray beyond this limit. Indeed there was a time when early stages of piano playing were spoken of as 'the drudgery' which had to be passed through before any attractive music could be offered. From a compass of five notes we moved, with triumph, to six notes and so on. Inevitably stiffness set in. One might as well teach a child to walk by keeping the legs tied together for the first few months! Today the most generally accepted method is to allow total beginners to play over a wide compass of the instrument. Many little exercises and pieces have been devised for rote playing. This does no harm providing reading at sight is also an essential part of every lesson and the reading compass is gradually extended.

With regard to the five-finger exercise, I myself am not happy about the 1.2.3.4.5 method. I feel it causes the hand to fall away on reaching the 5th finger and the hand position to lose its natural shape. In Book 1 of my *Freedom Technique* I open with a five-finger group moving between the thumb and each finger in turn (1–2, 1–3, 1–4, 1–5, and then back again). This promotes the beginning of rotary freedom (see Chapter 9), though the outward movement is so minimal we do not discuss it with the pupil. This exercise is followed by a series of short sequences to promote free movement in various directions. No. 2 is 'cross hand' (loved by young children), whilst No. 3 introduces 'arm weight and release' keeping the *fingers* firmly anchored to the keys. Exercise No. 4 moves over a wider range, each little group ending with a 'float off' to ensure easy freedom in *leaving* the key. Many pianists other than beginners tend to be 'keybound': you have only to place your hand under the forearm of one such performer in action to *feel* the tension in the lower forearm muscles. Trying to push the arm up is like prising a limpet from a rock! This continuous downward pressure is really damaging and precludes any hope of reaching a degree of technical proficiency. It *must* be eradicated in the earliest stages. Piano technique involves both exertion and release, and it is the *release* which is found more difficult. This is why I have made a point of it in many of my early exercises. Page 2 includes groups of paired slurred notes calling for a quick transference from one state to another, where the first note is, as it were, a downward stroke and the second an upward stroke.

I will not enumerate further the *Freedom Technique* exercises. Readers may have well-tried favourites of their own. All I ask is that any series chosen includes plenty of variety of movement, so that the beginning pianist does not become 'keybound' as I have described.

Much of what I have written above refers to beginning technique for we do have to appreciate that the teaching in early stages is responsible for much that is to follow. However, the ensuing chapters will, I hope, clarify many points for the more advanced student, the Diploma candidate, or even the teacher. From now on each aspect of technique will be discussed under a separate heading.

3. FINGER ACTIVITY

The fingers and thumb make direct contact with the keys and are the most continuously active elements in piano playing. For many years technical training tried to develop strength and agility by forcing the fingers against their natural physical condition. Nowadays, however, we take into consideration the contribution of hands and arms and of body-weight distribution. In this way we provide conditions that are helpful to the fingers, and they are able to work without the strain imposed on them by the technique of those bygone days.

Pure finger action starts from the knuckle and, without any added activity from the hand, produces only a limited tonal range. We can prove this by working the fingers independently. To do so, first depress a key with the thumb (this of course plays on its side due to its natural shape). Holding the thumb down, strike with each finger in turn a series of repeated notes. The fingers work as little hammers, approaching the note from just above the key surface and rebounding to the place from which they started. If the finger tips were to start their downward movement from the *key surface*, the result would be something like a hammer *pushing* a nail into wood.

Holding the thumb down in this way has a restraining effect on the arm and fingers and, if repeated too often, would result in tension just at the moment when it is not wanted, i.e. in the early stages. At a school where I once taught I came across a gadget on to which the arm was strapped. It was designed to hold the arm rigid, whilst the fingers alone did the work. Had there been such a thing as a pianist's 'chamber of horrors' I would have offered this to the collection!

Earlier I spoke of the hand and arm position as being 'equally balanced between shoulder and finger-tip'. This means that there must be *some* weight behind the fingers, even at the pianist's first attempts. This has been called 'resting weight' and is easy to describe if we sit with our hands resting on our laps. We can *feel* them there, but they do not 'push' into our legs or impose any weight on them. This resting weight helps in tone production and makes the early exercises less arduous than if we had to work from the knuckles alone.

The hand, unrestricted by a holding thumb, is able to move freely in any direction. Movement up and down the keyboard is controlled by the arm, which carries the hand to its destination. We have to be sure this is understood and that the hand does not have to drag the arm after it!

Though I suggested we do not restrict any beginner to a five-note compass, it was not with the intent of banishing five-finger exercises altogether. They are of course important in shaping the hand and getting the feel of the keys. Free from the 'holding thumb' the fingers are apt to become somewhat unruly in early stages. It is wise to keep the finger-tips close to the keys and limit the movement until the finger ends are strong enough to carry extra energy. To increase the tone a little we strike the key from a slightly increased height, but *at no point do we impose an upward lift after the key has been released.* Any upward movement from the knuckles is a *preparation* for the down and relative to the speed at which the key is to be struck. This is adjusted according to the tone required and can be compared with a golfer who adapts his backward swing to the length he needs to hit the ball.

The high-lifted finger was for many years looked upon as basic to technical achievement, speed, and facility. In my own copy of Bach's French Suites, used whilst at school, I see the words: 'Lift your fingers up' written large and clear. My teacher had been a grand-pupil of Clara Schumann, the finest woman pianist of her day. Outstanding performers of her time must have achieved their ends by sheer determination – or did they *unconsciously* free themselves of the acknowledged technique of the time without analysing just how they did it? After all, it is not likely that any great artist makes a mental note of every technical move throughout a performance. Imagine the brain keeping up a running commentary: 'Make sure my arm is light for this passage and increase the weight at the crescendo; prepare for rotary freedom in the next section; now add full arm weight, etc. etc.' How ridiculous that would be! The concert artist's technique is instinctive as a means to musical interpretation.

The following brief story illustrates my point. Some years ago I attended a Wigmore Hall recital given by the distinguished pianist Moura Lympany. She has kindly given me permission to recount this memory. At the end of the concert the usual crowd of friends and admirers made its way to the Green Room and one very earnest young man said: 'Tell me, Miss Lympany, how did you produce that lovely tone in the second movement of the Mozart? Was it with arm weight and a firm finger, or did you use a supported arm and finger touch?' Miss Lympany's answer was as instinctive as her technique: 'Really, I have no idea. I just play the piano and hope for the best!'

This is an ideal for the future, but in the student's progress much has to be learnt and *understood* before the ideal is reached. I cannot stress too strongly how important it is for *teachers* to be able to analyse technical movements, detect faulty muscular action, and build a secure technique for their pupils. Some performances that one hears in examinations and festivals *have* an air of 'hoping for the best'!

The wrist plays a large part in tone control and amount. It needs to be free and flexible to the immediate requirements of the music. It should never be 'flabby', neither should it be rigid. Exercises in Book 1 of *Freedom Technique* include one for 'arm weight' and release. The weight is added by the forearm and the fingers remain firm. This means the flexibility of the wrist controls the situation. More is written about what is often called 'arm weight' in the section on 'Cantabile' (pages 26–9).

Less accomplished pianists should play at a limited speed and aim to gain evenness of tone by using no more movement than is required to strike the key. When we are ready to use a bigger tonal range, we add energy from the hand, which together with the 'resting weight' of the arm gives scope for a crescendo or diminuendo.

At speed the fingers once more work close to the keys. As that very explicit technician York Bowen used to say: 'The quicker the closer'. What could be more apt? He was one of Matthay's pupils and an ardent enthusiast for his principles. He was able to explain their essence without the imaginative embroidery imposed on them by many who acquired a little knowledge second or even third hand.

Up to this point I have insisted that the arm's role in speed is only to support the hand and carry it to its destination. The virtuoso pianist, however, is able to use what we call 'constant arm weight'. This technique needs very strongly developed fingers and the ability to release all unused energy. The added arm weight does not involve visible movement; being constant it assists in tonal resonance and brilliance and is essential if glittering passages are to rise above a full symphony orchestra in a concerto. I mention this possibility with a strong warning: it can only be used by the virtuoso pianist. To add weight to weaker fingers, particularly at speed, would cause them to crumple and collapse.

This may be why some people seem to arrive at such harsh and ugly tone. Weight added by the less able pianist is produced by a series of jerks or prods into the key, driving it beyond the 'sound spot' which lies just above the key bed. This has been called 'key bedding', though the term seems not to be used very much today. But whatever it is called we have to avoid digging into the keys with a force that is totally unacceptable to the nature of tone production.

In the end we return to the point from which I started – control of the most active part used in piano playing, the end joint of the finger. This is the ultimate point from which sound is transmitted and there should be an instinctive liaison between it and the ear, in that the ear continuously listens and transmits correction to the finger. In my book *Interpretation in Piano Study* I refer to the 'listening finger'; this image is worth considering.

4. THE THUMB

Though everyone speaks of 'five-finger exercises', we have in fact only *four* fingers, the other member being the thumb. Due to its shape it works quite differently from the fingers, contacting the key with the side of its end joint. It has three joints; the one nearest the arm can almost be described as a continuation of the wrist and is able to do very little of its own volition. The middle joint is the most active, being capable of moving up and down or in a lateral direction. The end joint moves laterally only and its activity is essential in scale passages.

If you place the four fingers of one hand on a table top and, in imagination, strike a key with the thumb *unaided by any exertion from the arm*, you will find it has rather a limited downward power. To compensate for this the pianist has to use a *slight* push from the forearm towards the thumb end and this is where the trouble begins. The question is *how much* we allow the arm to participate. Over and over again inexperienced performers are said to have a 'heavy thumb', implying that it is the strongest part of the hand. This may be so in activities other than piano playing, but the thumb is not strong with the limited range of movement on the keyboard. The 'heavy thumb' is due to one of two reasons, (1) the use of too much assistance from the forearm, (2) too slow a reaction in the lateral direction when scale or arpeggio passages are played. This latter reason is fully explained in the section on scale playing (see pages 35–9).

To balance a melodic line, so that all sounds are of equal weight with no accent on thumb notes, requires careful and sensitive listening and adjustment. The thumb is an individual and sometimes rather an unruly one. The earlier the pianist learns this, the more likely he will be to keep it in proportion, according to the context of any music he may play.

5. LEGATO

Legato implies sounds that are joined or bound together. A textbook instruction as to how this is achieved is that the weight should be transferred from the bottom of one key to the bottom of the next. The fingers 'meet' at the bottom and do not pass each other on the way up and down as would a see-saw. It is like walking, one foot remaining on the ground until the next has reached it. This must cause a slight overlap which, though some technicians would have it otherwise, can be proved by playing two consecutive notes and depressing the pedal *at the exact moment* the second note sounds. Immediately we hear the dissonance caused by this proceeding. This chapter is not about pedalling, but the fact just demonstrated shows how dangerous it is to follow exactly the pedal directions in some otherwise reliable editions. Too often we see a 'Pedal down' sign at the moment a chord or note *within a legato phrase* is to be struck.

CANTABILE

Those who write or speak of 'cantabile' often imply that it only applies to certain passages. But surely we need to make the music 'sing' from the start, and as 'cantabile' means 'singing' it is not an art to be reserved for a later stage. The pianist will gradually learn to control the amount of energy used to control the tone and that a true 'cantabile' at slow speed is made by adding a little 'arm weight' to the fingers. In this the arm gently relaxes, allowing its weight to be transferred to the sound spot by a firm finger (*never* relax the finger tip).

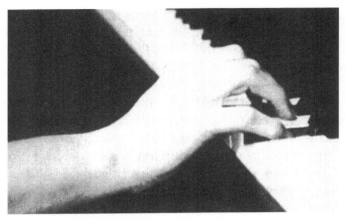

5 *Arm weight with firm finger tips (cantabile touch)*

To play a 'singing' melody, a row of notes at a moderate speed, the pianist moves from one 'arm drop' to the next with a *slight* outward swing of the elbow, bringing the arm up into a position to strike the next key. This creates a series of small circular movements, the right arm in an anti-clockwise direction and the left clockwise. The movement has a positive purpose in preparing the hand for what is to come. Unfortunately it has been grossly exaggerated; when the arm *jerks* outwards almost before the note has sounded, it hampers the tone because it causes the key to be released before the 'sound spot' is fully resonated.

This unfortunate style is not only detrimental to the sound but is so obviously imposed for 'effect' that it is very unpleasant to watch. It was this sort of thing – an exaggeration of the freedom taught by Matthay – that caused those who learnt of his principles second or third hand to decry them. In the same way that any upward movement of the finger is a *preparation* for the down, so this small outward swing keeps the arm in a condition of freedom in *preparation* for the drop at the ensuing point of finger contact.

Arm weight is of course essential in chord sequences. Combined with the use of the sustaining pedal we can get lovely rich sounds (see page 63).

A further problem for the pianist is to make a melodic line sing over supporting harmonies in the same hand. Added arm weight will not help in this instance as it would be transferred to *all* the fingers. Here we have to isolate the 'singing finger' and bring into positive action its end joint. This last joint, by added tension and exertion, projects the extra speed needed for the melodic line. If the melody is in the higher voice, it is the right-hand upper fingers that are active. It has been suggested to me that this line can be sung by tilting the hand outward. But what if the chord spans an octave or more and the hand is small? The thumb is already fully occupied and cannot be tilted away or it will not be able to play! It is certainly an indisputable fact that the advanced pianist needs to have the skill to isolate any finger at will. This is most apparent in the fugues of Bach, where the subject may be in the alto or tenor voice or even pass from one hand to the other. So it is *finger* exertion alone that can achieve this for us.

To return to a more elementary level I would like to offer a very simple exercise which, in teaching, I have constantly used with success for contrasting tone amount between one hand and the other. Taking a short scale, the notes played a tenth apart, we use 'arm weight' for the singing hand and very light 'finger touch' in the accompanying hand. The 'movements' are so contrasted that it is something like the game children play in which they stroke one leg and pat the other! Surely if they can do this, they can approach the keys in two different ways. It is so essential that 'notes' should become 'music' at the earliest possible stage, that I would recommend it as a 'first-term exercise'.

6. STACCATO

Staccato means literally 'detached', exactly the opposite of legato. The one big difference between the two is that legato has a constant definition whilst staccato can be interpreted in a number of ways from a very short sound to one that is only minimally detached. In this last instance staccato crotchets (quarter-notes) might be played as dotted quavers (eighth-notes) with quaver breaks. This interpretation, called 'mezzo-staccato' or 'portamento', is sometimes indicated on the printed page with slurred lines linking the staccato dots, but quite often it is left to the musical insight of the performer to interpret the staccato dot as it fits into the context of the music.

Let us consider the short staccato, the sort one would expect as a natural opposite of legato. It is not long since pianists were taught to achieve this shortness by loosening the wrist to a condition of flabbiness and flinging the arm back *after* each note had been struck, then bouncing back to the key surface. This meant that each time the key was struck the effort started at the key surface, and though this was possible at a slow speed, at a faster speed it was quite impossible. Having been taught this method myself I remember spending weeks conscientiously flinging my arm back whilst learning a study at a slow speed, only to be completely frustrated when I tried to quicken the tempo. The same happened later when I attempted octave passages (I write of these in Chapter 13). I felt I had been rescued and liberated when later tuition allowed me to do just that thing which had been barred in my early lessons. I had been told: 'Never *hit* the key.' Yet to play staccato or octave passages that is exactly what we have to do. Advanced pianists, of whatever technical school, could not possibly play cascades of octaves without doing just that!

Imagine, first, that staccato is being introduced to a beginner. What better way than to close the fall of the piano and, without even talking about such details as the condition of the wrist and hand, get the pupil to tap a rhythm as freely as he would knock on the door. When we knock on a door, we start from a little way away or we would not be able to make any sound. Having knocked, the hand with its flexible wrist bounces back to the place from which the knocking action started. So it is with staccato. Let the beginning pianist play his first staccato notes by using the middle finger and tapping out a rhythm on one note. He follows this by playing a scale from the outside to the centre using the 3rd finger – right hand downhill, left hand uphill. The reason for this is that it is the easiest natural direction for the hand and arm to move. Staccato is a kind of 'one-piece movement' involving an activity of the forearm and a flexible (but not flabby) wrist. There are some who consider we should tell those first attempting staccato to 'cease all effort at the moment the sound is made'. I wonder whether such instruction would really be understood by a young pianist first attempting a staccato touch!

Staccato has also been called 'hand touch'. This is because both hand and fingers act as one unit, the fingers having no independent down and up action. In very soft staccato the movement starts at the wrist. Beyond that the forearm takes control and adds more impetus as the tone increases, the wrist being flexible but never flabby. The role played by the fingers is at the point the key is struck. They obey an instruction from the brain that motivates whichever finger is to strike the key. This finger 'protrudes' towards the key and is carried there by the 'one-piece unit' of hand and forearm; the flexible wrist causes the rebound, whose height depends upon the speed and from what distance the movement started (see Plate 6).

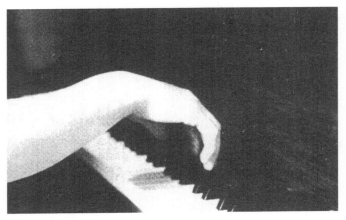

6 *Release from staccato*

In very fast staccato passages we have what is called 'finger staccato'. Here the music is too quick for the arm and hand to move with each stroke. The arm now reverts to a supporting role, whilst the fingers become active at the key surface and, as an exception to much that I have said, initiate a definite 'down and lift' movement. Obviously at speed they cannot lift far and the down stroke is played as though the key had become shallow, only just reaching the 'sound spot' before being withdrawn. This pure finger action cannot be loud. If 'presto-forte' is indicated the percussiveness of the piano mechanism *makes* the staccato for us and a normal 'speed technique' can be used with active finger articulation.

As I have already said, 'mezzo-staccato' is indicated by slurred lines between the dots. There are many instances where this kind of sound should be used though it has not been indicated by the composer. (The pianist has always to be alert to the kind of staccato that is suitable to the style and speed of the music.) Heavy, rich chords with a minimal break can be enriched by the addition of 'detached pedalling', the foot moving down and up in time with the arm. Here the visible arm energy is controlled by the wrist according to the amount of tone needed. This relates to 'arm weight touch':

If the music is soft and romantic in style, we often have staccato in which the wrist is more gently flexible and the fingers seem to leave the keys almost reluctantly – with young pupils I have described this 'as though there was glue on the finger tips!'

There are instances, particularly in free-flowing passages by Chopin or Liszt, when the sustaining pedal retains the resonance of the bass under a group of staccato notes. In this instance the fingers move lightly over the keys, being supported and guided by the arm. There is no deliberate 'down and up' movement:

32

Pedal changes are also used to sustain bass notes, even if marked staccato, in instances such as this:

Schubert frequently writes staccato dots over melodic lines or bass accompaniments that would sound completely wrong were the pedal not added:

A further consideration is the isolated staccato note appearing at the end of a fluent legato phrase:

Here, since the movement towards the staccato is smooth there can now be no question of striking the key from above. Staccato, in this instance, implies the instantaneous release of finger and pedal. The finger can be said to 'float off', but *not* with a flabby wrist. Were it possible to 'freeze'

the moment of release the arm would be seen to support a relaxed hand, the fingers dropping down towards the keys and the 'staccato finger' still slightly protruding. (Again as in **Plate 6**.)

Though the use of pedal is not the main theme of this chapter it has been included in the last few examples to demonstrate the many implications of that rather insignificant-looking little dot.

There are, of course, occasions when an imposed upward 'spring' does become necessary. In the following short excerpt from a Beethoven sonata, the wide leap is more easily negotiated at the rather fast speed required if the initial note (B flat) is treated as a 'springboard' from which the arm is impelled upward to the octave F by a powerful 'kick off' from the hand and fingers. I have indicated an arc to try and show the line of flight:

A further case for this upward 'thrust' is when an anacrusis leads to a strong staccato chord:

In my earlier book on interpretation I have offered a wide variety of possibilities. The main object of this chapter is of course technical, but interpretative matters have been bound to creep in. Nevertheless I hope this section will help to clarify some of the technical requirements of the many possible varieties of staccato.

7. THE LATERAL SWING

To move laterally is, of course, to move sideways. Our hands need to do this with ease if they are to cover the span of the keyboard. Movement in any direction starts with the arms, which support and carry the hands. So a lateral swing is an *arm* movement. To create the conditions of lateral movement place the hand over a table top, with the 3rd finger touching the surface. Keeping this finger firmly anchored swing the arm outwards away from the body and then back towards the thumb. It will be obvious that the outward swing is more pronounced than the inward. The elbow takes with it the upper arm and the 3rd finger acts as a pivot from which the hand swings. This movement is used to a greater or lesser degree in the performance of scales, arpeggios, widely spaced broken chords, and also when chords beyond the span of the hand are broken or 'harped'. Let us take these contingencies one at a time.

SCALE PLAYING

All pianists have to learn scales, not only for technical reasons but to gain a knowledge of key and chord formation. Though the subject matter of this little book is technique I cannot resist stressing that a knowledge of key through scales is an integral part of musical knowledge without which no pianist is a *musician*.

The basic necessity in scale playing is a smooth movement of the thumb as it passes under the fingers. In describing how smoothness can be achieved I am referring to the right hand ascending, the thumb being the starting point. Of course the movements apply equally to the left hand descending. The first movement of the thumb should present no visible or *audible* effort and preparation for this is made *before* the initial note has been struck. As the hand prepares to play, the elbow swings away from the body, causing the fingers to lie obliquely over the keys and the thumb to be in a position ready to move. Immediately the first note has been struck with the thumb, it moves under the second finger rather than back to its normal resting position. From then on it travels continuously, always being in position when needed.

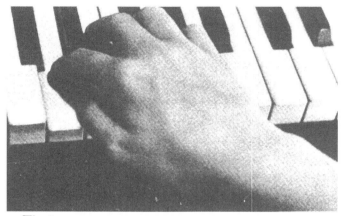

7 *The 'moving thumb' in scale passages*

The travelling thumb is carried along by the outward-moving elbow, which in its turn is supported from the shoulder and assisted by a free body movement to the right. This I referred to when discussing the sitting position and I have often encouraged my students, *in practice only*, to play a rapid four-octave scale with one hand while keeping the head and eyes as nearly as possible over the travelling fingers. This is an exaggeration of movement but helps to promote a really free body balance.

It is easier to play the scale back towards the centre. The

elbow can be said to be 'led home' by the hand, though in actual fact the arm still supports the travelling fingers and guides them by gently pushing instead of pulling.

Perfection in scale playing implies complete equality of tone and controlled finger articulation. Advanced students, reaching a greater speed, can add brilliance by increasing the tone towards the top octave. This will compensate for the natural loss of resonance when the thinner high strings are struck.

At this point some will be asking: 'What about scales in contrary motion?' Obviously the body weight in these has to remain central, but as they are never asked for over more than a two-octave register, the *elbow* will still be able to assist the hand in its outward movement.

Having suggested an ideal, I have to admit that those of us who work in the examination field sometimes hear scales that are far from ideal. The most common faults are:

1. Uncontrolled thumb turn, due to the pianist *starting* the scale with the hand lying at right angles to the keys with the elbow returned to this tucked-in position after each thumb note. This results in a series of jerks and a very audible 'bump' when the thumb plays.
2. Scales played slowly with a separate arm-weight action for each note. I call this the 'pump-handle' method and it is impossible to reach even a moderate speed with this kind of foundation.
3. White key notes played near the edge of the keyboard necessitating a forward lurch for every black key.
4. High-lifted and over-round fingers, probably with caved-in knuckles. From this stiff and unnatural beginning no future facility will be possible.

It is essential to introduce a natural basic scale technique from the start since movements once formed become habitual and are difficult to alter. Any teacher receiving a pupil who already plays scales with any of the faults listed above should explain and demonstrate the difference between ease and awkwardness and treat scale playing as a priority.

Some scales present greater problems than others, having awkward corners to negotiate. Typical are B, B flat, and E flat harmonic minors. It can be helpful to isolate the awkward notes for repetitive practice. In the examples that follow the fingers play well forward on the keys:

Scale practice need never be dull. Here are some suggestions for the student:

1. Rhythmic variations. I give three here which appear in *Freedom Technique* Book 3. Their value lies in the necessity for quick exertion and release, the shorter note values calling for a quick release of the natural 'resting weight' from the arm.

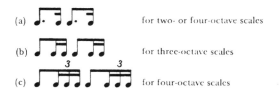

2. Dynamic contrasts. These could be with both hands simultaneously playing crescendo and diminuendo, or with the hands working each in its own way – one staccato the other legato, one forte the other piano, and so on. When 'cross time' such as 'two against three' has to be learnt, scales can again be used. (Note that if triplets are in the left hand it will need to start two octaves below the right or it will overtake it!)

3. The teacher can ask for scales by their key signature (very valuable in minor keys) or to be started on a note other than the tonic.

Single-hand scales in thirds are not included in this section as their technical approach is quite different. Reference to these is on pp. 47–9.

ARPEGGIOS

Arpeggios at slow to moderate speeds require a more pronounced lateral swing than do scales because the thumb has further to travel. There are two lateral movements to each octave, one to take the thumb under and the other to bring the fingers back over the thumb. At the risk of being repetitive I underline the necessity for a sitting position that enables the body to move with the hand and the arm, especially remembering to be well forward on the stool. It is surprising the number of students, some quite well advanced, who have come to me with somewhat sticky arpeggios and have shown immediate improvement when I have changed their sitting position.

Ideally 'four-octave arpeggios' should be heard in groups of four. If the arm and thumb are heavy, we will hear the white key chords with an accent on each thumb, resulting in groups of three. Exercises for ease in arpeggio playing are helpful to avoid misaccentuation. This one comes from *Freedom Technique* Book 3:

to be played also in the left hand and in ALL KEYS

Having to span a wide distance, the fingers cannot be curved as in scale passages. If we stretch the hand widely we will find that the fingers flatten naturally. No teacher should insist on round fingers in arpeggios.

The foregoing applies to arpeggios at a slow to moderate speed. Were examination candidates in the lower grades to make a visible and audible 'jump' at the thumb turn, the examiner could well comment on it. When however a high speed is called for, the approach is totally different. At a tempo approximating to presto it is impossible to perform the gyrations of continuous quick lateral movements – these would be awkward and hampering to fluency. Here we have reached a point at which the arm travels outward at speed but without lateral swing. It remains level and moves in one piece with the fingers, the elbow moving up and down in line with the hand and *the thumb* being continuously active laterally. It might be argued that there will be no legato by this method, but at great speed the line between legato and staccato no longer exists. One cannot tell *audibly* that the line is broken because the fingers and thumb are now almost percussive, the hand muscles activating them towards a clear and evenly articulated arpeggio. In this way real brilliance is attained and, as in scales, a crescendo towards the top adds to the brilliance.

WIDELY SPACED BROKEN CHORDS

Broken chords are often included as an accompaniment, especially in music of the Classical period. They can be of the Alberti Bass shape or spread across the keyboard. Those of the Alberti Bass are included in the section 'Rotary Freedom', but those that move straight up or down require lateral freedom if they are to be played with ease. To attempt a continuous flow with a fixed arm results in stiffness and unevenness. This causes the notes to be bunched into groups, thus:

The cure may be found in practising the move from the final note of one group to the initial note of the next:

From this exercise the groups are gradually joined until the whole becomes even. A similar exercise occurs as No. 30 of *Freedom Technique* Book 3.

Beethoven often introduces broken-chord groups for the left hand. Here is the opening of the development of Sonata Op. 14, No. 1:

Beethoven

From these comparatively simple groups we move to wider spacing which requires a far greater lateral swing:

To practise the above play first the central notes, the interval of a minor 3rd – E and G. Holding these two notes firmly down swing back and forth between the outer notes, A sharp and C sharp, repeating the wide 'swing' many times. This can only be accomplished with complete lateral freedom which leads to an easy movement across the span. (See Plates 8–9.)

41

8 *Start of lateral swing in the left-hand passage of Beethoven, Op.14, No.*I

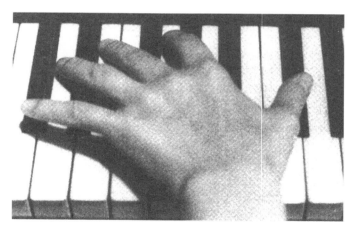

9 *Completion of lateral swing towards the thumb (above passage)*

HARPED OR SPREAD CHORDS

Methods of practice will be the same as for widely spaced broken chords, the central note acting as a pivot. Exercises are introduced in *Freedom Technique* Book 3. An ideal piece for practice is 'The Elf' from Schumann's *Albumblätter* using the central note of each hand as a pivot:

Schumann

This example from a Chopin Mazurka, having only a single spread chord, seems to cause a break in the performance of younger students:

Chopin

At the point marked * we encounter the problem. The student in many cases dives down to low C forgetting that this causes him to lose all contact with the G he has just played. If, however, the 3rd finger remains anchored over the G whilst aiming for the low C all the fuss is eliminated and the thumb can swing onward and upward to the E flat. I would like to quote one further passage, this time from a much played Chopin Waltz. The example is from the second section:

In the left-hand part the first two bars lie under the fingers but the third does not: it demands quite a spread for the hand. The central note of the spread chord, being only a tone away from the B flat, should be approached first by a neat downward movement with the 2nd finger. Firmly in place, it acts as a pivot between the low B flat and the D and the situation becomes quite easy.

LATERAL MOVEMENT WITHOUT VISIBLE SWING

Having argued the case for lateral swing, I have to accept that, as in very fast arpeggios, widely spaced passages require speedy movement without lateral *swing*. Wide leaps are made easier if the note immediately before is treated as a kind of springboard. By 'taking off' from the initial note the arm and hand are propelled 'in one piece' in whichever direction they have to travel. This is made easier if the arm describes an arc rather than remaining close to the keys. Exercises for this kind of 'aerial travel' are much enjoyed by younger pianists and give a freedom which is impossible if their early technique is confined to a five-note compass. Here is one from *Freedom Technique* Book 1, followed by another from Book 3:

(a) Right hand alone

(b) Left hand alone

repeated chromatically and in each hand, the left hand starting from the centre outwards.

The same type of 'volition' is used in the Beethoven example on page 34 to travel from the B flat to the octave F. All wide leaps are easier if there is an active 'spring' from the taking-off point.

8. CHROMATIC SCALES

Given the right technical conditions chromatic passages can be played with considerable speed, even by pianists of modest ability. It all depends upon the relative position and balance between fingers and thumb. The standard right-hand fingering from C – 1.3.1.3.1.2.3.1 etc. – shows how vital is the thumb's role. To find the ideal balance we strike the D flat with the third finger and, without allowing any visible drop of arm or hand, gently play C with the thumb. Two essential points emerge. The thumb's contact with the key can be no further than the side of the nail (normally it makes contact up to about half the joint) and the fingers become slightly flattened, striking their keys about an inch forward from the thumb.

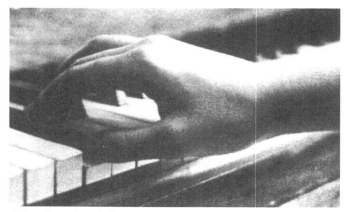

10 *Thumb and 3rd finger in position to begin a chromatic scale*

This description has not appeared in any technical book that I have read. One writer insists that we play chromatic scales with rotary movement, but I have experimented at the keyboard and cannot find how this can be done except at a very slow speed.

Arm support is vital and the elbow leads outwards and follows back as in diatonic scale. One could describe the movement as 'gliding' with absolutely no visible alteration in the height of arm or hand throughout the scale. Any fussiness from the thumb will cause uneven tone and general insecurity.

9. CONSECUTIVE THIRDS

Higher Grade examinations ask for scales in thirds and the **LRAM** Diploma for scales in double thirds. There are several ideas on the technical approach to them. The one I have to offer ensures evenness of tone and the least amount of fuss when the thumb passes *over*. This passing over is diametrically opposed to the passing *under* in normal scale passages, so, in the first place, we need to play with the arms at right angles to the keyboard.

Assuming the 'Double thumb' or 'two-group' fingering, we have in the right hand, starting as an example with

$$\begin{array}{llllllllll} \text{E:} & 3 & 4 & \overline{5} & {}^2 & 3 & 4 & \overline{5} & 3 & \text{etc.} \\ \text{C:} & 1 & 2 & \underline{3} & 1 & 1 & 2 & \underline{3} & 1 \end{array}$$

I have marked the awkward moments. The tendency when passing from $\frac{5}{3}$ to $\frac{2}{1}$ is to push the elbow right in turning the hand sideways.

Apart from the difficulty and tension set up by this manoeuvre, the pianist is likely at an increased speed to release the third finger preceding the turn and finish up with $\begin{smallmatrix} 3 & 4 & 5 & {}^2 & 3 & 4 & 5 & 3. \\ 1 & 2 & & 1 & 1 & 2 & & 1 \end{smallmatrix}$

As double-third scales are not expected to be at a great speed, I have found it helpful and completely adequate to instruct my students, in the initial lesson, to use a minimal arm weight and release for *each* third. Care is needed to ensure a legato between both voices, except at the turn when it is obvious one of the two notes has to be released.

The turn is made by swinging the $\frac{2}{1}$ or the $\frac{3}{1}$ over the fifth finger *keeping the arm at right angles to the keys*. It is obvious the lateral muscles must be very flexible and free and the scale made to sound as legato as possible (unless staccato is asked for!).

In *Freedom Technique* Book 3 there is an exercise for introducing this scale, first in groups, then as a whole. One of the most challenging sections finishes thus:

The fingering of the scales, though always in two groups, needs patient study and has to be built up over a period of time. The pattern I suggest can be got on a 'Matthay Scale card' or in the Associated Board published book of scales as one of two alternatives.

CHROMATIC THIRDS

Once the fingering has been mastered, chromatic thirds are easier to play than diatonic thirds. Going outwards is easier than coming back. I have found it helpful to write the fingering as for a contrary-motion scale, the right hand beginning on E flat and G flat and the left hand on B flat and D flat. Here it is:

$$3\ 4\ 3\ 4\ 3\ 4\ 5\ 3\ 4\ 3\ 4\ 5\ 3$$
$$2\ 1\ 1\ 2\ 1\ 2\ 1\ 2\ 1\ 1\ 2\ 1\ 2$$

It will be realized that the outer fingers supply the legato, and it is a good idea to start with these fingers on their own (again from the same part of the keyboard): 3.4.3.4.3.4.5.3.4.3.4.5.3. Playing a chromatic scale with this fingering brings the elbow fairly close to the body. It is, incidentally, a fine preparation for the type of finger movements often required in the music of Bach.

Returning towards the centre is found a little harder. The main thing to know is when to play the 5th finger. In the right hand it is on the upper of two adjacent white keys, F and C. With the left hand it is E and B. The contrary-motion practice suggested seems to help in this respect.

Technically we do not need the same arm energy as for diatonic double thirds. These chromatic scales can be played with the smoothest possible finger touch on their outer legato parts.

10. ROTARY FREEDOM

The working of the rotary muscles was perhaps the most revealing and, at the same time, the most misrepresented of Matthay's principles. I will try to explain in simple terms what we mean by rotary movement and rotary freedom (the two not being synonymous).

A most enlightening explanation of the principle of rotary freedom came from a candidate for the Teacher's LRAM. I was on a board at the time when one of my most distinguished colleagues, Vivian Langrish, was asking the questions. He had a unique way of 'becoming the pupil' so that one really did begin to think he *was* the pupil. On this occasion he started to play the Allegro from Beethoven's 'Pathétique' Sonata, struggling manfully with the left-hand broken octaves and finally giving up through sheer stiffness and tiredness. 'Why can't I play these?' he asked. 'I have practised really hard and they get no better.' The candidate, an intelligent woman in her mid thirties, was more than ready with a solution. 'You can't move freely,' she said, 'because your rotary muscles are locked.' Mr Langrish looked mystified. 'Could you explain clearly what that means?' 'Oh yes,' she said, 'it's because you were made to climb trees and so your arms were put on this way' – here she demonstrated a tree-climbing act – 'so when you turn them inward to play the piano it causes tension in the forearm. To relieve this tension you rotate the arm outwards causing the hand to tilt towards the little finger and then swing back again'. Needless to say the candidate passed, and I have visions of strings of little boys and girls being told they were 'made to climb trees'!

What more can I add? The basic facts cannot be better described. We do impose tension of the muscles of the inner forearm when we lift the hand into position over the keys and it is only by swinging away from the centre that we release that tension. Matthay used the word 'rotary' which stems from the Latin 'rota' – a wheel. What the pianist does is to turn the wheel a very short distance.

The two terms 'Rotary Freedom' and 'Rotary Movement' are not quite synonymous, though part of technical vocabulary. It remains for me to explain the difference between the two.

A simple illustration of rotary *movement* can be got if we clench the fist (not tightly) and lay the hand on the table. If we place it down in the position in which it naturally falls from the shoulder, it will lie on the little finger only. To move into a position for playing the piano, we swing the forearm inwards and cause the thumb also to contact the table. We have made that swing with the rotary muscles and they will remain in a condition of tension so long as they have to hold the thumb inwards. It will be found almost impossible to move further towards the thumb end without involving unnatural gyrations from the shoulder. However it is quite easy to swing the arm outwards, so that once more only the little finger rests in the table. It follows

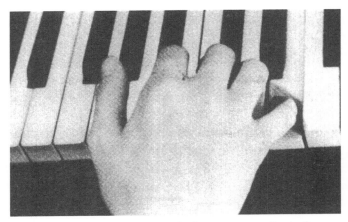

11 *Outward rotary swing with firm contact of 5th finger*

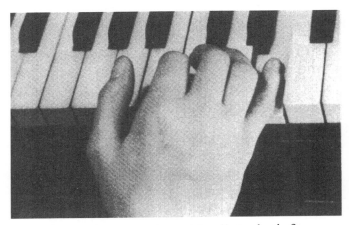

12 *Outward rotary swing with collapsed 5th finger*

then that what we call rotary movement in piano playing is an outward rather than an inward swing.

As a preliminary introduction this kind of 'in and out' swing can be performed on a table top or across the three adjacent black keys of the piano.

Exercises to ensure the rotary muscles are freed through

gentle movement could be introduced in the early stages of piano playing. Nos. 1 and 6 in Book 1 of *Freedom Technique* have this in mind. Here is No. 6:

In Book 2 the same idea is extended, but could well be given to any beginners who have a suitable hand:

The accents marked are important, because of the need to soften the constantly repeated notes. Young pianists who play sonatinas with an Alberti bass often do so with a heavy left thumb. This reiterated note *must* be softened. The style is typical of 18th-century music, including the sonatas of Haydn and Mozart. Here are a few bars from Haydn which, had I included the whole section, would involve 40 repetitions of the note A. Imagine the effect if it were not lightened!

A few bars later the right hand takes over the semiquavers, and plenty of rotary movement towards the upper notes is needed. The staccato marks indicate accents. In inserting them Haydn wanted to ensure softer notes at the thumb end:

During my teaching life students of some ability have come to me having no mental or physical concept of the need for rotary freedom through movement. For them my invariable choice is the Prelude No. 15 in G from Book 2 of Bach's 48. It is an ideal study, offering almost continuous rotary movement to either one hand or the other:

(a) Right hand bars 1 and 2   Bach

(b) Left hand bars 4 and 5

The most testing passages needing complete freedom of rotary muscles through movement are those containing a series of broken octaves. A musical example is not needed here, but anyone approaching the coda of Beethoven's Sonata Op. 2 No. 3, first movement, will have severe problems if the forearm is stiffened. Such passages need drive and continuity which can only be attained through ease and freedom of the forearm.

It would appear by what I have just written that there is little, if any, difference between rotary movement and rotary freedom. This problem was presented to me many years ago when I came across a question in a teaching paper for ARCM candidates: 'What is the difference between Rotary Movement and Rotary Freedom?' I have to confess that at the time I had to do a lot of thinking before the disarmingly simple answer came to me: 'Rotary movement is visible, Rotary freedom does not have to be visible.' Freedom is part of the natural state of the arm for which we hope and about which I wrote in Chapter 2. There I said, in talking of relaxation, 'we relax any muscles not needed for the job of the moment': most of the time the rotary muscles come into this category. You can tell whether they are free by simply placing your hand under the forearm of a pianist whilst in performance. The tightening of such muscles can be felt in the hardness of the arm. Ask a pianist whose muscles feel tense to play a one-octave scale in either hand outwards from the thumb and, when he or she has reached the fifth finger, put your hand under the thumb end of the forearm and try to swing it outwards away from the centre. You will find that the arm resists your pressure and pushes against your hand. If the rotary muscles are free the arm will respond and swing outwards.

The only occasions when the rotary muscles have to go into a condition of firmness are for octave passages (not broken) or strong 'martellato' chords.

On this subject I would like to give a final word of warning. Rotary movements must *not* be made at the expense of finger technique: the fingers themselves must remain firm, especially the 5th (see Plates 11 and 12, p. 48). This was one of the perversions of Matthay's principle which was taught by those whose knowledge came to them second or even third hand. It caused teachers of the old school to frown on any ideas of freedom and continue to insist that their pupils play all passages as with a coin balanced on the back of the hand!

11. REPEATED NOTES

By tradition repeated notes are played with finger changes. The reason is fairly obvious. If we try to make a number of quick repetitions of one single note using, for example, the 3rd finger, we will find tension quickly building up in the forearm from which the movement is initiated, however flexible the wrist may be. The arm, being the heaviest member concerned with putting down the keys, cannot maintain a series of quick oscillations without becoming increasingly stiff and tired.

Finger changes are taken from the outer fingers towards the thumb. Thus, a three-group series would have 3.2.1.3.2.1. etc. and groups of four 4.3.2.1. This rule seems to puzzle those who attempt to make such changes with the arm held forward from the body instead of obliquely. If the arm is held at right angles to the keyboard an attempt at quick finger changes can be awkward and *looks* awkward, because the fingers are having to work hard from the knuckle to 'get out of each other's way'. If the elbow is allowed to swing outwards away from the body it will be found that the hand can assume a position in which the fingers can 'share one key', each using a different part of it, the 4th finger furthest forward and the thumb near the edge of the key. In this way the arm only has to *support* the fingers whilst the oscillations are made from a flexible wrist (see Plate 13).

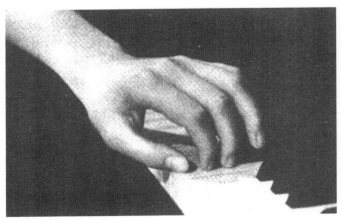

13 *A helpful arm and finger position for quick repetitions on a single note*

55

Finger changes are also advisable where one note has only two quick repetitions. In the two examples that follow the slur effect (softening of second quaver) would be impossible unless fingered as marked.

For slow repeated notes it must be a matter of personal preference, though I myself think it is easier to maintain an even tone if changes are made, possibly only between the 2nd and 3rd fingers. Where the repeated notes move at a moderate speed, as in the middle section of Chopin's D flat Prelude, I feel finger changes to be essential. Whatever method is chosen the arm plays a vital part in controlling the tone.

Freedom Technique Book 3 gives exercises for quick changes, but, as I have just indicated, no exercise need be added for slow repetitions.

12. TRILLS

To me it is impossible to lay down an exact technique for trills because so much depends upon the shape of the hand, particularly the length of the fingers. It is obvious we need to have the fingers completely unhampered by weight from the arm *or hand* and not *lifted* above the striking point. In first attempts at trill passages the danger lies in an effort to produce excessive speed. A trill, being literally a repetition of two adjacent notes, can even be on the slow side, particularly in the works of Bach and composers of the Baroque period. It is better to modify the number of notes in a trill than to allow it to displace the pulse. For this reason *early* attempts need to be modest in their speed.

Normally one trills from the knuckle, and it is for this reason I refer to the length of the fingers, particularly the length from the middle joint to the finger end. If this section of the finger is held in a condition to work independently, my remarks about speed playing (page 23) apply here too. The instinct in most cases is to confine trilling to the second and third fingers. But, apart from the fact that this is not of necessity the 'easy' way, there will one day be instances where other trills are demanded, even between the 4th and 5th fingers.

For a start I would recommend trill passages to be attempted between 1.3, and 2.4 and finally 3.5. Adjacent fingers offer by no means the most flexible solution. In long trill passages it is helpful to change the pairs that are working. The hardest pair, 3.4, need rarely if ever be used, but anyone who wants to scale the heights of Beethoven's third-period sonatas will need to be able to trill with the 4th and 5th fingers.

In *Freedom Technique* Book 3 an exercise is given which uses each pair of fingers in turn. In this one must not forget the *left hand* – perhaps not so often called upon to trill, and therefore when its turn comes showing a marked reluctance to vie with its stronger partner.

A well balanced piece of music, demanding trills in alternating hands, is the Prelude in G minor from Book 1 of Bach's 48. This music does not demand brilliance in its trills, but requires equal ability between the hands. In the Haydn F minor Variations, the trill section of Variation 2 also calls for left-hand trills which must be as brilliant as those in the right.

On the whole I find it successful to teach young pianists to approach a trill with the wrist just a little lower than is normal, but I have also seen brilliant trills played from an unusually high wrist. Providing the fingers feel easy and the rotary muscles are completely free, the trill technique should gradually improve.

In the end, as in normal fast playing, the added brilliance required for advanced work, particularly the cadenza trill in a concerto, takes some added energy from the hand muscles and even, in a highly developed and powerful technique, from the arm.

13. OCTAVE PASSAGES

There are many pianists in the intermediate stages who seem to think there is some kind of special art in the performance of octave passages which is unsurmountable unless the pianist is about to mount the concert platform as a professional! Far from this, once the hand has grown to a span of just over an octave the technical demands are almost indentical in the initial stages to those I suggested as an introduction to staccato. The preliminary exercise of rapping out a rhythm on the closed fall of the piano, using an action as though to knock on a door, can apply equally at an octave span. A good technical foundation for octave playing, whilst the hand is growing, is to extend the same action to thirds, played with the 2nd and 4th, and then to sixths, played by thumb and 5th. Each 'rapping' episode is followed by a scale at the appropriate interval. For the small hand the performance of scales in sixths is no different from octaves for a large hand!

In each instance the scales are first played softly, keeping the movement close to the keys, the arm supporting the hand, and the drop towards the keys being from a flexible wrist. As the tone increases the forearm begins to take a more active part, but the wrist should never stiffen completely.

Extending this to the octave, it will be noticed that the wider the span of the hand the more we lose the bend of the *last* fingerjoint, and the more the upward curve is at the wrist rather than at the knuckles. The hand, supported by the forearm, falls in one piece from the wrist (see Plate 14):

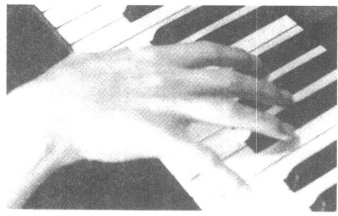

14 *The octave played well forward on the keys where the stretch allows*

and, were a full chord to be played instead of an octave, the weight would be conveyed to the keys via a one-piece unit of the *two* last finger joints, the 'bend' being at the middle joint.

Octave passages should become part of the technique as soon as the span has reached a little *over* an octave. As soon as possible the student must learn to play well forward from the edge of the keys so that passing quickly from black to white does not cause jerks. In early attempts there is a temptation to 'bounce back' to the key surface before striking the ensuing octave. This must be checked at once if there is to be any hope of increasing the speed. It is something I myself know only too well, for I was allowed to attempt octaves in just such a way and the ensuing frustration led me to impose on myself a really drastic exercise as a cure. This method I pass on to my own students who have any sign of the 'bounce and wait' method, but *I must stress it is only a 'kill or cure' idea* and not the ideal way to learn octave technique! However it seems to do the trick, so I offer it here.

The plan is to 'attack' the octave from well above the key surface – say about 6 inches – and immediately after striking it, to rebound to the original starting position, at the same time closing the fingers into the palm of the hand. From that position we have literally to 'pounce' upon the next octave, the hand instinctively opening as it drops to encompass the interval. A series of octaves played this way will certainly start the cure and before long the hand drops to the key from a normal position.

The method of attack suggested here can well be used in the practice of consecutive chord passages – those in the cadenza of the first movement of Schumann's Piano Concerto come to mind, though it is not likely a pianist who has reached this stage will need such a drastic approach. However the point at issue is that *any* chord, large or small, that is to be played staccato must be 'shaped' within the hand before the keys are struck, and it is an interesting and challenging part of practising to 'think of a chord', and then immediately pounce on it from above.

Octave playing poses a hard problem for those whose hands remain small when fully grown. It is a sad truth that, however much early promise is shown, a limited hand span is a drawback at an advanced stage. Flexibility and plenty of exercises for stretching the fingers will help a lot, but when the hand is so small that octaves have to be played 'on the edge of the keys', quick movement from black to white keys is almost impossible. The small hand, too, remains flat in its effort to reach the octave and this will mean a low wrist (see Plate 15).

Though I have implied that in the initial attempts to play octave groups, as in early staccato, the hands should keep close to the keys, more energy and arm movement is needed as confidence is gained and as the demands of the music increase. Brilliant and fast octave passages need all the energy that can be summoned up without accident! The arms in a real forte take over almost entirely, the minimal flexibility of the wrist supplying the final 'punch' towards the keys. Such passages are often performed in a way that is truly spectacular to the audience and the fingers need to be immensely strong to take all the weight that is imposed on them. Perhaps it is the experience of watching such brilliance – especially if close up on television – that makes the more timid pianist shrink from the idea of learning music that embodies octave passages. If he could begin in the modest way offered here, he may reach a better octave technique than he expected.

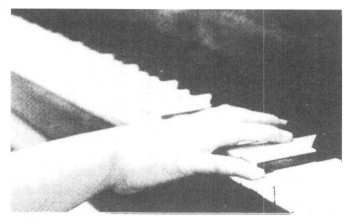

15 *The problem of playing an octave when the hand is small*

14.   PEDALLING

When writing about the mechanism of the instrument I described the way in which the dampers work with the hammers, leaving the strings as the note is struck and returning to them when the key falls back into its place. When the sustaining pedal is depressed the dampers are lifted from *all* the strings and remain in this condition until it is released. Thus to hold a pedal down over a series of disharmonies will result in a confused jumble of sounds. But, used with correct foot technique, allied to an understanding of harmonic texture, pedalling adds greatly to musically satisfying effect. It is a sad fact that this very sensitive mechanism is so often given only scanty thought and used in a haphazard way, when the exact moments of depressing and lifting are as important as the moments when notes are played.

The first use of the pedal is to join sounds that cannot be reached with the fingers, but it has a far wider effect upon the sound. It adds richness and beauty to the tone and, as the pianist becomes aware of its many potentials, skilful pedalling highlights phrasing and adds an almost ethereal 'cloudiness' to soft music in the upper register of the piano. It should never be called the 'loud pedal'.

Just as the action and weight of the keys feel different on different pianos so do the weight and resistance of the pedal. For this reason the pianist needs to get the feel of the pedal before playing on an unfamiliar instrument. The heel should remain on the ground whilst the ankle works to move the sole of the foot up and down on the pedal surface.

If we depress the pedal and play a full arpeggio to the top

of the piano we will notice that even the highest strings continue to vibrate though they have no dampers to them. This is due to 'sympathetic vibration' and demonstrates the sensitivity of the damper mechanism.

The first practical approach is through what is called 'legato pedalling'. As an introductory exercise a scale could be played using only the 3rd finger, making the *joins* with the pedal. The foot goes down when the initial note is struck and then, *by listening*, we release the pedal *at the moment the next sound begins to be heard*. It is then put down again *as soon as the dampers have done their work*. The sentences in italics must be clearly understood. There is no other method for 'legato pedalling'. The habit of 'snatching' at the pedal with monotonous regularity, whatever register of the instrument is in use, is to be decried. Those who do this have not paused to think that the long, thick bass strings vibrate for a greater length of time, and therefore the foot must *stay up* for longer so that the dampers *remain on these strings* for sufficient time to dampen their sound. Once the sound is dampened then the foot again works downwards.

From single notes we move to chord progressions. Hymn tunes can be useful for practice. Ideal pieces in the Classical repertoire are the Chorale from Schumann's *Album for the Young* or, in the case of more advanced students, Prelude No. 20 in C minor by Chopin.

Exact coordination between ear and foot needs quicker reaction in music such as given on pages 32–3 of this book. When the left hand moves quickly to and from low bass notes it is all too easy either to make the change too late and lose the bass altogether, or to snatch at it and leave go too quickly, resulting in a blur between the previous harmony and that which is just beginning. Such passages need practice with the left hand alone coordinating with the pedal. Results can only be got by always *listening and criticizing*.

A useful but less common method of pedalling is 'staccato' or 'detached' pedalling. In this the hands move up and down exactly with the foot. This does not make a legato but it enriches the tone of big and fairly slow chord passages that are indicated as detached. A good instance of this has already appeared in the Schubert example on page 32. For obvious reasons this type of pedalling is not attempted until legato pedal has become instinctive and secure.

For further uses of the pedal, including 'half pedalling', 'half damping', and 'flutter pedalling', see my *Interpretation in Piano Study*.

15. FINGERING AS AN AID TO TECHNICAL FACILITY

Fingering may not seem to come within the context of technique, but its choice has a strong influence on the facility of certain passages. This is not the place to consider the generally accepted rules for the fingering of scale passages, broken or grouped chords, or widely spaced notes. Neither do I propose to enumerate the problems of 'finger changes', moving obliquely up or down the keyboard, or sliding from black to white key.

The purpose of this chapter is to show how a collaboration between mind and finger at certain points can be assisted by writing in fingers as 'signposts'. To scatter the copy with innumerable fingering marks is futile and unnecessary, but a few well-placed marks can act as points of definition towards which a phrase may flow or from which it may start. Even in such things as scales and arpeggios, a practice method such as the following might be introduced:

Some students find it difficult to coordinate the hands when playing chromatic scales a minor third apart; there can be a tendency to drift into major seconds or major thirds. By concentrating on the *fingers* from which the scale started the student can move from one octave to the next and arrive with security, gradually building up the register to four octaves. Let us say the scale starts from C (L.H.) and E flat (R.H.). Concentrate the mind on left-hand thumb and right-hand 3rd finger, knowing that these two fingers must meet at the octave. 'Thinking rhythmically' we play as fluently as possible towards that meeting place, pause there, *then use it again as a starting point*. The rhythmic shape for this type of practice will then be:

If one asks the average teacher how a pupil should practise quick passages the answer will, almost invariably, be 'slowly'. In essence this is true and very sound advice, but it cannot be the only answer. Monotonous slow practice involving a number of repetitions of the same phrase is bound to cause boredom unless it is combined with an observance of dynamic variation and phrase shape as in the musical text. A further reason why excessive slow practice is unadvisable is that the pianist is almost bound to combine the slow playing with added arm weight, thereby individualizing each note instead of moving towards a point. This is where my 'signposts' can help. Here is an ornamental run from a Chopin Nocturne. I give it here with the 'signposts' written in large type. A few necessary intervening fingers are also written. The complete run is followed by a second example, suggesting how the student might move (as fast as he or she can) from one 'signpost' to another:

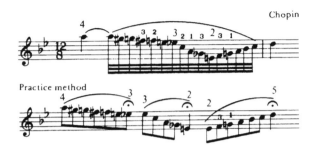

Here is a left-hand section taken from one of Mendelssohn's 'Songs without Words'. It, too, is followed by a grouped practice method.

These 'points of arrival' have even more significance where the hands move quickly in unison. This section from a Gigue by Bach could well be taken from the first note of each bar to that of the next, then again started *from that point* and continued in the same way. When this has been accomplished two bars are welded together, and so on until the phrase is safely under the fingers.

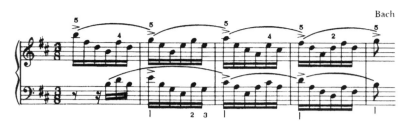

Bach

Lightness of arm is essential when groups move quickly over an extended area of the keyboard. In the following the slurred pairs of notes are graded tonally by 'arm weight and release', the first of the two being on the down stroke. It is helpful to write finger indications over the first of each pair so that the student has a visual image of what might be called the operative points, the weight passing from one point to the next. The faster the music moves the more difficult this becomes with those who are not advanced technically. The Allegro from Beethoven's Op. 31, No. 2 demands this kind of control and it may be found necessary to practise it slowly with an exaggeration of the weight on the first note of the two. Being marked at an Alla Breve tempo it moves really quickly:

Beethoven

This last quotation might appear to be too closely related to the examples on page 56 but the purpose behind the fingering indications is to move on one step to a *tonal* effect. In fact, the same principle could be applied to these examples.

Fingering concentration again helps to 'tighten up' slack rhythmic sequences containing dotted notes. So often the note following the dot arrives too early and with too much weight. In long passages the dotted rhythm often begins to sag. Once more fingering and sectional practice come to our aid. It is a good plan to exaggerate the length of the dot, or even to pause on each long note value and precede to the next as an acciaccatura. Obviously this is only for practice purposes and not to be included in performance! The example that follows will illustrate:

A fast passage containing intermittent extensions can also be practised from point to point whilst intervening fingers move with minimal weight. From Beethoven's Op. 10, No. 1 we have a sequence that seems to worry many aspiring pianists:

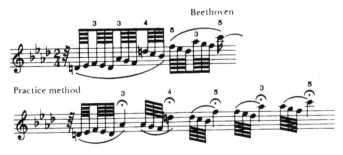

from this, two, then three, then all groups are joined up. Again the point of rest was on a predetermined *finger* to which and from which the other notes flowed as quickly as possible.

All pianists must study rudiments and harmony, and

they should relate their knowledge to the keyboard or to whatever music they may be learning. It is, obviously, a real aid to memorization. In the Beethoven example on page 56 the falling broken chord is built on an E flat major triad, in that on page 68 the initial and final note (and therefore the repeated notes) of each group is part of a D minor chord. It can be helpful to break up passage work into block chords. Here is the introduction to a Chopin Waltz, basically the chord of E minor, each inversion being approached from a semitone:

Students find this phrase from Beethoven's Op. 22 difficult. Being built on the chord of B flat major it should receive similar practice.

In all these instances correct fingering guides the fingers towards the operative points and concentration on these leads to technical fluency.

A BRIEF RESUMÉ FOR TEACHING-DIPLOMA CANDIDATES

This does not presume to be fully comprehensive. No one can predict the workings of the minds of *all* examiners nor their preference for certain answers. But, from my own experience, it should contain enough to satisfy the average examining board.

The examiners will probably ask whether you have already given piano lessons. It is no disgrace to answer 'Yes', but this answer presupposes a sound knowledge of basic technique so it is as well to have it! A very usual question is how you would conduct a first lesson to a beginner. Commendation would be given for an answer that shows interest in any music-making the pupil has already experienced, either at school, in a choir, or by participation in an ensemble of some kind. This leads to the various ways the sound can be made. These are then related to the piano, which is in fact a 'tuned-percussion' instrument. Further information may be requested about the mechanism of the instrument. These need not go beyond key, hammer, soundboard, damper, and, of course, the strings. All answers should be clear and succinct and anyone who meanders round the point may lose marks.

There will probably be questions about the best sitting position and hand shape. It is important to know that the *shoulder* lifts the hands to the keyboard. This simple bit of information seems, at times, to elude candidates.

Questions on technique can be asked directly or by illustration – the examiner puts deliberate faults into his performance, asking the candidate to criticize and correct any point which appears to be faulty. I opened this sentence with 'questions on technique' because that is the main purpose of this book, but of course it is *vitally important* that wrong notes or faulty time be corrected before commenting on such things as poor tone or blurred pedalling.

Wrong notes *should* be easily detectable, as they are normally inserted into the works the candidate has just played, but the ear sometimes plays strange tricks when we are nervous and wrought up and the most blatant faults can be allowed to pass by a candidate who is expecting something very subtle about tone production or technique. I give here two typical examples from standard Diploma works. In each the correct text is followed by the inaccuracy.

Beethoven, Op. 10, No. 1, bars 3 and 4
CORRECT INCORRECT

(a) Correct

Beethoven, Op. 14, No. 1, Allegretto

(b) Incorrect

Mistakes at ✳

It is, perhaps, less easy to detect the inversion of broken chord accompaniments but this kind of mistake will probably be made one day by your pupils so always listen carefully to such passages.

(a) Correct

Beethoven, Op. 14, No. 1

(b) Incorrect

(a) Correct

Beethoven, Op. 10, No. 1

(b) Incorrect

Another mistake that can be introduced, perhaps having a slight 'catch' as in this example, is to omit notes:

(a) Correct

Mozart, K.576

(b) Notes omitted at *

Omitted notes appear in greater profusion in the next example, yet because they don't sound too bad an anxious candidate may need a second hearing (this is always given).

74

When rhythmic faults are played the candidate needs not only to detect them but to offer a solution for their correction. This, invariably, lies in counting the subdivisions of the beat and the candidate may choose to count crotchet bars in quaver beats (8 counts for 4/4) or to offer 'One-and, Two-and,' etc. Either are acceptable. On the next page are two opening phrases, the first by Beethoven, the second by Mozart. In each the correct text is followed by a possible mistiming.

Time faults need close attention when triplet quavers are played like this: ♪♪♪ This fault is fairly prevalent and one might offer Beethoven's Op. 49, No. 2 as an ideal piece for moving from triplets to duplets and back. Cross time, especially 'two against three', should be clearly understood. The common rhythm is clapped *as passing to the next beat* and the duplet is fitted *exactly half way* between the second and third note of the triplet:

Faulty tone distribution will have an unrhythmic effect on music that is otherwise played in time. The opening of

(a) Correct, subdivided as quavers   Beethoven, Op. 10, No. 2

(b) Incorrect

(a) Correct   Mozart, K.576

(b) Incorrect

Right-hand part only

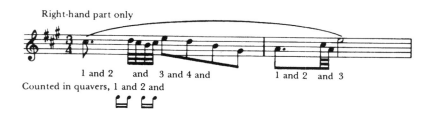

1 and 2   and   3 and 4 and   1 and 2   and 3
Counted in quavers, 1 and 2 and

Beethoven's Op. 10 No. 1 (below) or of the Allegretto from Op. 14, No. 1 (see page 73) will lose the 'tightness' of their rhythm if the shorter note values are not softened.

Beethoven, Op. 10, No. 1

The candidate should be able to demonstrate practice methods at all levels. Particularly valuable are those shown on pages 41 and 69. Criticism needs to be constructive rather than destructive. It is no use detecting a fault unless there is a way of rectifying it.

Technical faults will, I hope, be detected and corrected if this little book has achieved its end. I will summarize these as briefly as possible.

LEGATO

Described as sounds that are joined or bound together, the most acceptable answer is that it is like 'walking'. The possibility of a slight 'overlap' can be demonstrated by using the pedal as I described earlier. All may not agree but a positive approach clearly demonstrated is always respected.

STACCATO

A normal lead to this question will be for the examiner to select a staccato passage from the prepared work and play it with flabby wrist resulting in a high arm movement. The answer relates so closely to the section I have devoted to staccato (in the first instance) that there is little to add. It should be made clear that, once the key has been released and the dampers have returned to the strings, further exertion is both waste of energy and a contributor to inaccuracy. So 'keep closer' to the keys.

SCALES

The candidate should know how soon he or she would introduce them (as soon as the pupil has acquired an adequate legato) and what is their purpose. They have a twofold purpose, one being musical and the other technical – neither should be omitted. The turn of the thumb involves a slight lateral movement but the important thing is to demonstrate how quickly it should move under, directly it has played.

ARPEGGIOS

Make sure to use the term 'lateral' in connexion with these. Explain that the arm carries the thumb under and the fingers over, *the thumb does not drag the arm along*. If asked about arpeggios at a really fast speed demonstrate how a lateral swing can no longer apply.

CANTABILE

This is most likely to be introduced by the examiner who will select a phrase, probably from an adagio movement, and play it with thin and unresonant tone. The candidate should immediately comment that the music does not 'sing', in fact it has no 'cantabile' tone. Asked how this can be got, say that it must be introduced through 'arm weight', and be sure to know that this involves relaxation of weight from the arm but *firmness at the finger ends*. Candidates who are not sure about this can get really muddled *if any further questions are forthcoming about* RELAXATION. Remember *we only relax the muscles not needed for the job of the moment*. Some may ask whether the arm falls further for a soft or loud sound. This, of course, brings in the state of the WRIST which, being constantly flexible to the need of the moment, resists the weight earlier and falls *less far in loud tone*.

ROTATION

This principle, so aptly described by a one-time candidate, was one of the most important 'aids' clarified by Matthay. It stems from the fact that the arm is not falling in its natural position when playing the piano and that ease from tension can be got by rotating it away from the centre. In demonstration, watch the examiner carefully in his performance of broken octaves, sixths, or any other passages where rotary movement could help. These I have described in detail. It would be as well to know that rotary *movement* is visible though rotary *freedom* – more constantly called for – is not, and that the rotary muscles are in the forearm, not the wrist.

SPEED

The examiner is almost certain to select a passage requiring technical facility and play it with one or other of the salient faults. In the first of these the performance will be clumsy and uneven, the whole appearance being one of effort and the wrist dangerously low. Many candidates will say that it is uneven and the wrist held too low, but what the examiner is wanting is: 'The arm is too heavy, it must be lifted (or lightened). With all this weight behind them the fingers are bound to crumple up and collapse. Arm-weight touch must not be used for such passages.'

A further faulty demonstration could be with high-lifted fingers, causing a thin and 'spidery' touch because the fingers are snatched from the keys before they have reached the 'sound spot'.

PEDALLING

The last chapter in this book gave any detail the candidate needs to know. If asked 'What is the function of the pedal?' the answer is 'First to join sounds that cannot be reached with the fingers and secondly (and equally important) to enrich the tone. Asked 'When do we change the pedal?' answer 'Normally at a change of harmony, but other conditions such as phrasing also play a part in determining this'. A demonstration or explanation will be expected, and I repeat that, if playing a series of notes or chords, the pedal goes down with the first, is lifted *as the next sound is heard* (*not* 'when the next note is played') and put down again *as soon as the dampers have done their work*. For an explanation of this last answer turn back to the chapter on pedalling.

Beyond the many technical points enumerated in this book the candidate will need to have a knowledge of repertoire. Such a subject does not have a place in a book about technique so I will only suggest that the student becomes familiar with music from all periods, especially from the works of the great masters who have written for the young. It is also essential to know of the study and sonatina composers and to be familiar with works in the modern idiom. Quotations can be limited to the opening bars – it is not necessary to know whole works from memory!

In all, the examiners look for lucidity, quickness, and common sense rather than long, erudite meanderings. I hope this book will have served in some way towards this ideal.